UNSOLVED

ESCAPE FROM ALCATRAZ

DINAH WILLIAMS

Children's Press®

An imprint of Scholastic Inc.

A special thank-you to our team of fact-checkers.

Library of Congress Cataloging-in-Publication Data available

ISBN 978-1-5461-7856-9 (library binding) | ISBN 978-1-5461-7857-6 (paperback)

10 9 8 7 6 5 4 3 2 1 26 27 28 29 30

Printed in China 62

First edition, 2026

Book design by Kay Petronio

Photos ©: cover: Sebastien Tabuteaud/Getty Images; back cover background: FernandoAH/Getty Images; back cover top: Andrea Pistolesi/Getty Images; 1: Sebastien Tabuteaud/Getty Images; 2–3: FernandoAH/Getty Images; 4–5: Caroline Purser/Getty Images; 6: Jim McMahon/Mapman ®; 7: MBPROJEKT_Maciej_Bledowski/Getty Images; 9 all: Bureau of Prisons; 10: GGNRA/Park Archives/GOGA19200–259/National Park Service; 11: SF News/Newspapers.com; 12: Andrea Pistolesi/Getty Images; 13 top left, top right, bottom left: Federal Bureau of Prisons; 13 top center: Bettmann/Getty Images; 13 bottom center, bottom right: U.S. Department of Justice/Wikimedia; 14: Jet Lowe/Library of Congress; 16: Bettmann/Getty Images; 17: Bettmann/Getty Images; 18–19: AP Wirephoto/Sydney Morning Herald/SuperStock/Alamy Images; 20: FBI; 21 poster: FBI; 21 inset: Federal Bureau of Prisons; 22 left: FBI/Wikimedia; 22 center: US Federal Government/Wikimedia; 22 right: Wikimedia; 24: Golden Gate National Recreation Area/National Park Service; 25: Tom.k/Wikimedia; 26: Robert Alexander/Getty Images; 27: Golden Gate National Recreation Area/National Park Service; 28: Liz Hafalia/San Francisco Chronicle/AP Images; 29: Golden Gate National Recreation Area/National Park Service; 30, 31, 32: FBI; 33, 34 top: Golden Gate National Recreation Area/National Park Service; 34 bottom, 35, 36: FBI; 37: Tayfun Coskun/Anadolu Agency/Getty Images; 38: AP Images; 39: History Channel; 40: Jay Hare/The Dothan Eagle/AP Images; 42 foreground: Reuters; 44 top left: DanHenson1/Getty Images; 44 top center: AP Wirephoto/Sydney Morning Herald/SuperStock/Alamy Images; 44 bottom left, bottom center, bottom right: Federal Bureau of Prisons; 45 top left: MBPROJEKT_Maciej_Bledowski/Getty Images; 45 top right: Reuters; 45 bottom left: Andrea Pistolesi/Getty Images; 45 bottom right: History Channel; 46 top: Sipa/Shutterstock.

All other photos © Shutterstock.

CONTENTS

INTRODUCTION: Escape the Rock 4

CHAPTER 1: Missing 8

CHAPTER 2: A Failed Attempt 12

CHAPTER 3: The Plan 20

CHAPTER 4: A Daring Getaway 32

CHAPTER 5: Manhunt 38

What to Believe? 42

Timeline: Then and Now 44

One Criminal, Three Escapes 46

Glossary 47

Index 48

About the Author 48

INTRODUCTION

ESCAPE THE ROCK

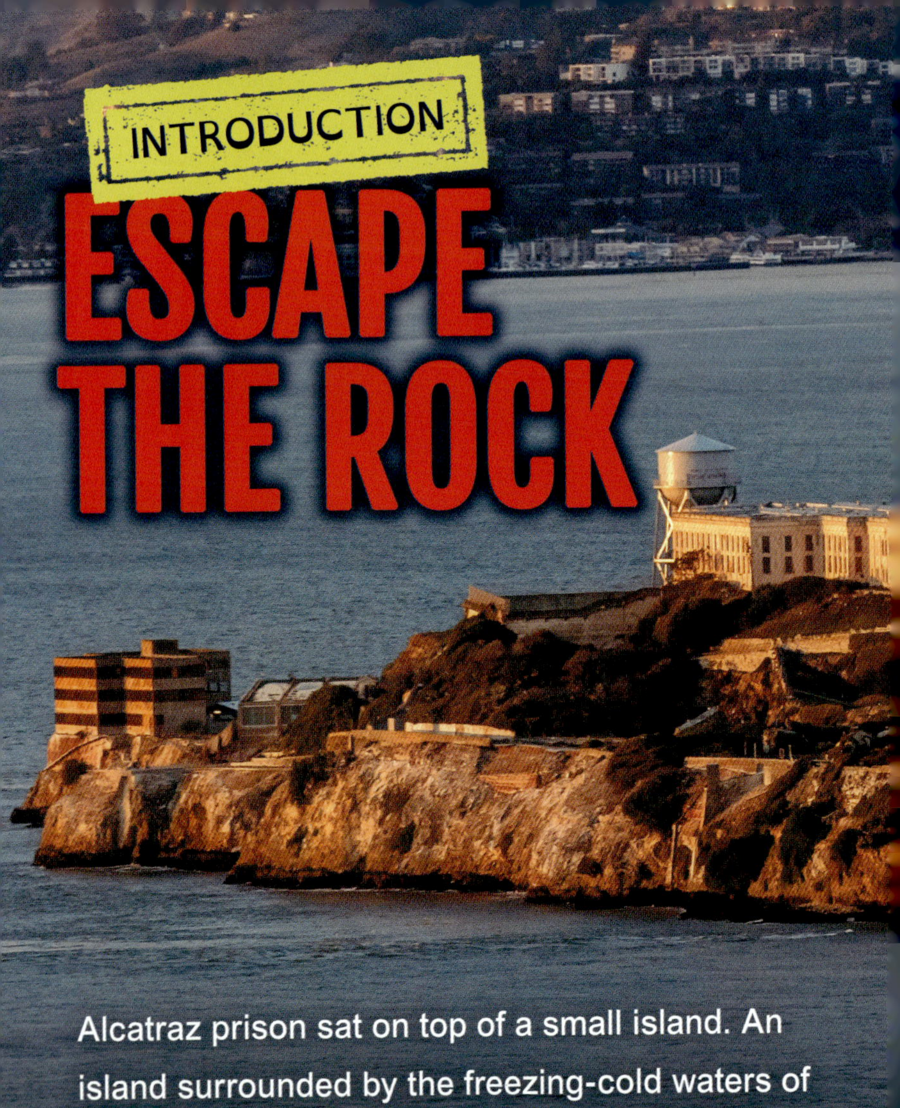

Alcatraz prison sat on top of a small island. An island surrounded by the freezing-cold waters of San Francisco Bay. The stone prison had high walls. Guards watched the prisoners' every move

Some of the most dangerous criminals in America were sent there. Why? Because Alcatraz was supposed to be escape-proof. Any attempt to escape would likely end in failure—or worse!

Alcatraz operated as a **federal** prison from 1934 to 1963. One of its famous **inmates** was the gangster Al Capone.

Alcatraz Island is about 1.5 miles (2.4 km) from San Francisco's shore.

Alcatraz became known as "The Rock." It looks like a pile of rocks in the bay.

While Alcatraz was open, thirty-six inmates tried to escape. Some were recaptured. Some were killed by prison guards. Some made it down to the water. And some were never seen again.

Did they drown in the strong currents of San Francisco Bay? Or did they really make it to freedom? Let's explore three daring attempts to escape from Alcatraz!

CHAPTER 1

MISSING

Theodore Cole and Ralph Roe were bank robbers. They were both caught and sent to prison. Both also tried to escape from prison. That's one reason they were sent to Alcatraz in 1936.

This is a main hallway inside Alcatraz. It is lined with cells on both sides.

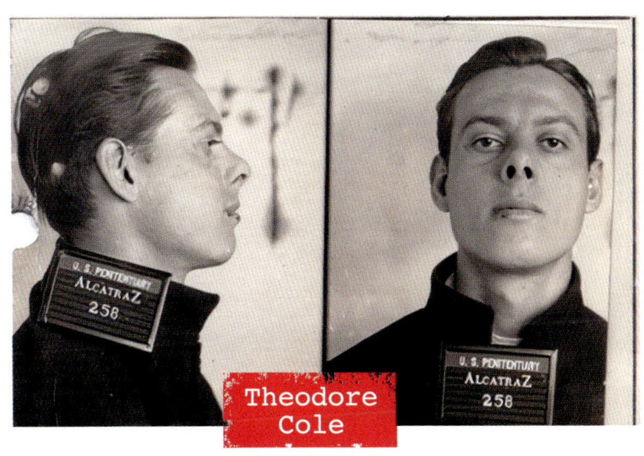

Cole and Roe both had prison jobs. They made rubber mats from tires. They were working together on December 16, 1937. A guard took a head count of the prisoners at 1:00 p.m. Cole and Roe were there. The guard took another head count thirty minutes later. The two men were gone.

This is the workshop where Cole and Roe worked.

The guards began searching for the missing inmates. They discovered that the bars and glass on the workshop's window had been cut. The inmates had squeezed out of it. The men used a wrench to break open a gate. The gate led out to the water. But what happened next?

Cole and Roe must have gone into the water. The fog was thick that day. Maybe that's why no one saw them. The currents in the icy water were strong. Could they have made it to the opposite shore? Their bodies were never found. No one knows if their escape was successful.

A newspaper printed that Cole and Roe drowned. But we do not know for sure.

The San Francisco News

FIRST Financial Race News

PRICE FIVE CENTS

SAN FRANCISCO, FRIDAY, DECEMBER 17, 1937

'DROWNED IN BAY'

That's Alcatraz Felons' Fate, Searchers Believe

EAVIEST FOG N 20 YEARS BLANKETS CITY

AT HIGHEST MARK

'HEROISM EVERY AMERICAN CAN BE PROUD OF'

ABOARD U. S. GUNBOAT OAHU, at Shanghai, Dec. 17.—The sinking of the United States gunboat Panay by Japanese airplanes added a heroic chapter to the history of the American Navy. The Panay went down fighting gamely to the end. Her men were at their guns, some smeared with blood from

SPROUL HINTED IN LINE FOR BIG G. O. P. JOB

University of California President Reported Giving Matter Serious Thought

NO COMMENTS MADE

QUARRY IN GREAT MANHUNT

FOG HAMPERS LAND, SEA HUNT FOR CRIMINALS

SHORE LINE PATROLLED

Theory of Accomplices in Boat Off 'The Rock' Is Discounted

CHAPTER 2

A FAILED ATTEMPT

Bernard Coy robbed a bank. He was caught and sent to Alcatraz in 1938. Eventually, he was assigned a job as a janitor. This job allowed him to walk around the prison. Coy noticed that the guards had routines. He watched them for weeks. He knew when they would come and go.

Coy also watched how the keys were used to unlock the cells. He came up with a plan to escape. Five fellow inmates also went in on the plan.

These six men planned to escape from Alcatraz.

It was May 2, 1946. That day, Coy knew there wouldn't be many guards in the **cellblock**. Coy and Hubbard overpowered one guard who was on patrol. They stole his keys and locked him in a cell. Coy unlocked the cells for Carnes, Cretzer, and Thompson. Coy then had to get into the gun gallery. This was the only area with an armed guard and weapons.

This is a view of the cells from a third floor guard station.

The gun gallery at Alcatraz.

Coy knew that the bars around the gun gallery weren't strong. He had made a bar spreader to bend them. Coy squeezed through. The gallery's guard returned. Coy attacked him. He stole guns and ammunition. Then he forced another guard to release Shockley.

A guard looks up at where the six men were trapped.

The six men planned to go out the front door. It led to the prison yard. They'd use the guards as shields so they wouldn't get shot. Then they would steal a prison boat and escape to freedom.

But Coy couldn't open the front door. The guard's keys wouldn't work. Now the six inmates were stuck in the cellblock. More guards kept coming to find out what was happening. The stuck inmates shoved the guards into cells. But even more guards came. What were they going to do?

This is the front door in Alcatraz. The inmates couldn't open it to escape.

The six inmates took more guns from the guards. They decided to shoot their way out. Cretzer shot five guards. More guards who tried to enter were also shot. Two were killed. The head of the prison called the US Marines to help. The Marines freed the trapped guards that night.

The Marines used grenades to free the guards. Smoke poured out of the windows.

Coy refused to surrender. The next day, the Marines opened fire on Coy and the other inmates. Coy, Cretzer, and Hubbard were killed. Shockley and Thompson received death **sentences**. Carnes received a life sentence. This violent incident was later called the Battle of Alcatraz.

CHAPTER 3
THE PLAN

Frank Lee Morris

Frank Lee Morris's parents died when he was eleven. He soon started to get in trouble with the law. He was arrested for the first time two years later. He found himself in and out of jail throughout his life.

ESCAPED FEDERAL PRISONER
FRANK LEE MORRIS

Photographs taken 1960 FBI No. 2,157,606

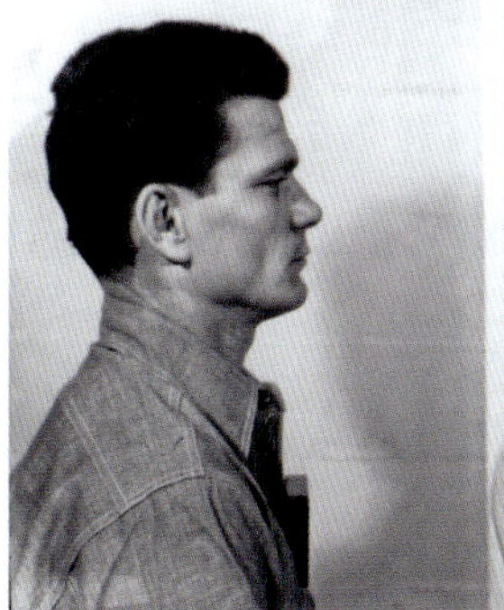

Aliases: Carl Cecil Clark, Frank Laine, Frank Lane, Frank William Lyons, Frankie Lyons, Stanley O'Neal Singletary, and others

Morris was thought to be very intelligent.

Morris then got caught after he robbed a bank. He was sent to prison in Louisiana for ten years. He tried to escape and was sent to Alcatraz in January 1960.

Morris's cell in Alcatraz was near Clarence and John Anglin's cells. Next to the brothers was Allen Clayton West. Those three men had also tried to escape from prison before. That was part of the reason they had been sent to Alcatraz.

The four inmates soon began to talk about how to get off the island. They knew it wouldn't be easy. It would take a lot of planning and creativity. But they had nothing but time to make a plan.

Clarence Anglin

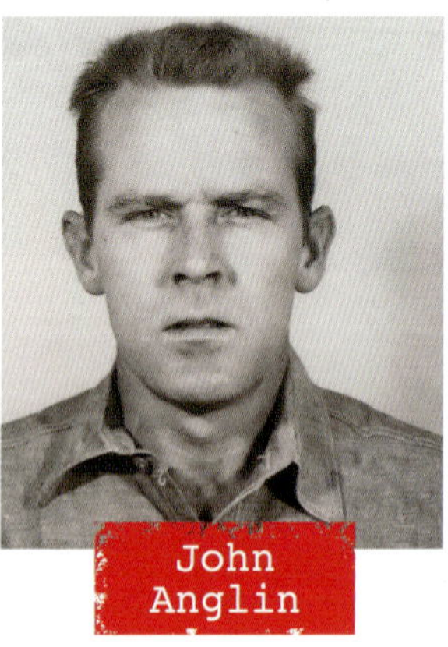

John Anglin

Allen Clayton West

MAKING MUSIC

Prisoners at Alcatraz who followed the rules could earn privileges. These could be visiting the prison's library, having a job, or playing music. Morris was allowed to play the accordion. He played in the evenings. This helped him carry out his escape plan. His music would hide the noise the other men would make.

Morris's accordion sits on his bed.

The men learned that there was an unguarded hallway. It was located behind the air vents in their cells. They started digging around the vents. They used spoons they stole from the dining hall. West also made a drill out of a broken vacuum cleaner.

They quietly chipped away at the concrete walls around the vents. They would flush the chips down the toilet. Or they would take them outside in their pockets. It took months for the men to get the vents off.

West had asked to fix the broken vacuum.

This is the unguarded hallway discovered by the inmates.

The vent hole was hidden during the day.

Two men would squeeze out of the vents into the hallway at night. The other two would keep watch and work in their cells. They set up a workshop in the empty hallway. That's where they started building everything they needed to escape.

Morris figured out how they would get off the island. He read in a magazine about how to make a raft and life jackets out of raincoats. The four men stole fifty prison raincoats and got to work. They also built a paddle for the raft.

This is a *Popular Mechanics* magazine article. It showed Morris how to make a raft.

Four fake heads like these were discovered after the escape.

Morris knew they needed time to carry out their plan. He slowly gathered soap, cotton rags, and toilet paper. The inmates took paint from a crafts class. They also took hair clippings from the barbershop. They used the materials to make four heads that looked like them.

The fake heads would be put in their beds on the night of the escape. That way the guards wouldn't know they were missing until the morning.

The inmates also planned to use fake bodies in their beds. They would place towels and clothes under their blankets.

The plan was to escape through the roof. But the men still needed to figure out how to get up there. The walls in the empty hallway were 30 feet (9 m) high. So, they climbed up pipes to get to the ceiling.

These are the tools and materials left in the hallway.

The men used this roof vent to escape.

There they found a vent. They used the tools they had to chip away at the space around it. Finally, they were able to get it open. The vent led to the roof. That's when the men decided it was time to put their plan into action!

CHAPTER 4

A DARING GETAWAY

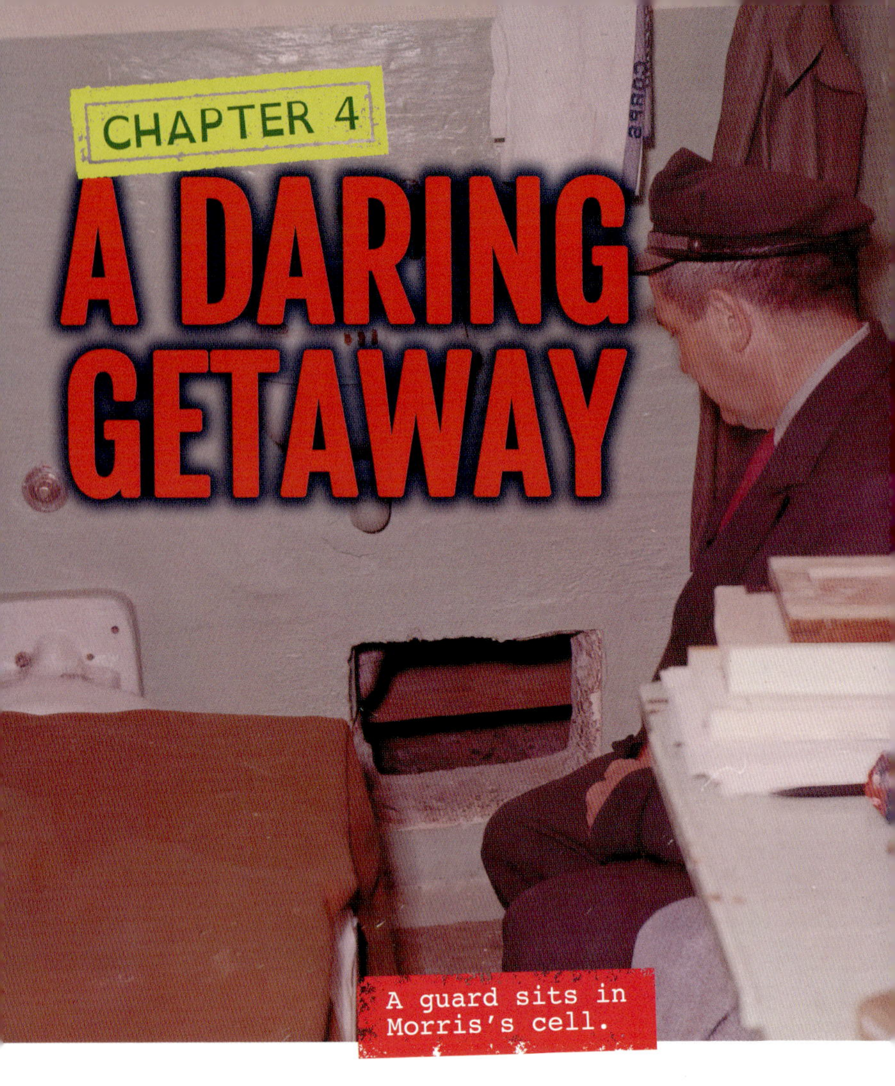

A guard sits in Morris's cell.

The night of June 11, 1962, was foggy. The prison guards called “Lights out!” at 9:30 p.m. Morris told the others it was time to go. The men put the fake bodies and heads in their beds.

But West couldn't open his vent! It was stuck. Clarence tried to kick it in from the other side. It wouldn't budge. They had no choice but to leave him behind. West managed to get through his vent, but it was too late. The other inmates were gone.

One of the escape holes is examined by a guard.

This is the rubber raft made from raincoats.

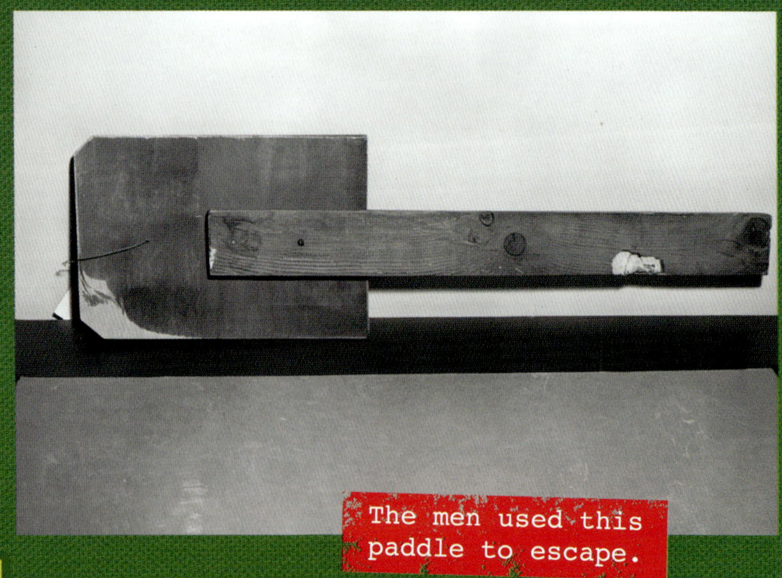

The men used this paddle to escape.

Morris and the brothers made it onto the roof. They ran across it with their raft and life jackets. Then they made their way down a pipe to the prison yard. They climbed over the fence and made it to the water's edge.

The plan was to paddle the raft north to Angel Island. Then they would swim from Angel Island to the mainland. There they would steal a car and clothes and split up.

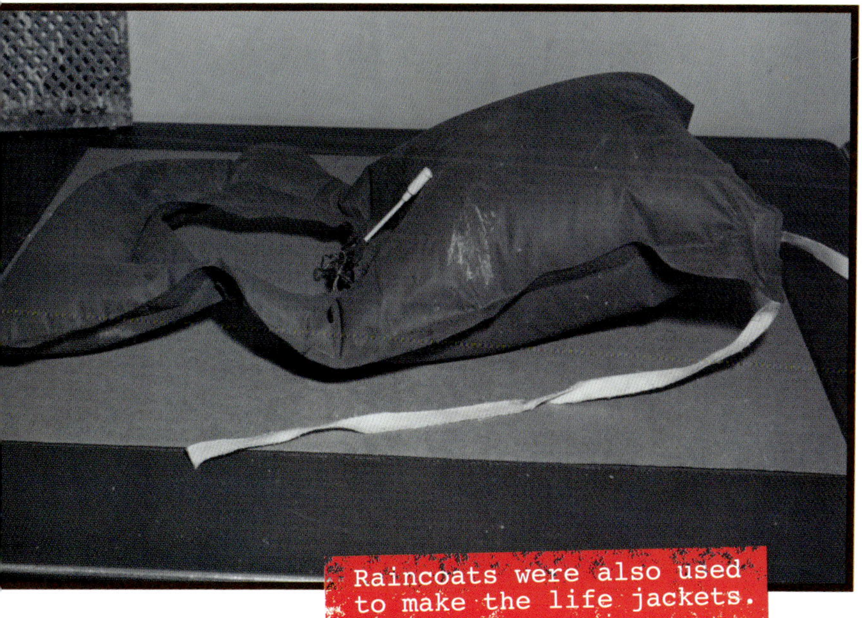

Raincoats were also used to make the life jackets.

The next morning, a guard went to wake up Morris. When he nudged the body in the bed, the fake head rolled off the pillow. He had escaped! The guards soon realized that John and Clarence were also missing. The prison went into **lockdown**.

The search for the escaped prisoners began. The head of the prison called in the **FBI** and the US Coast Guard. The guards soon discovered that West's vent had been opened. They took him in for questioning. West eventually told them about their plan to escape.

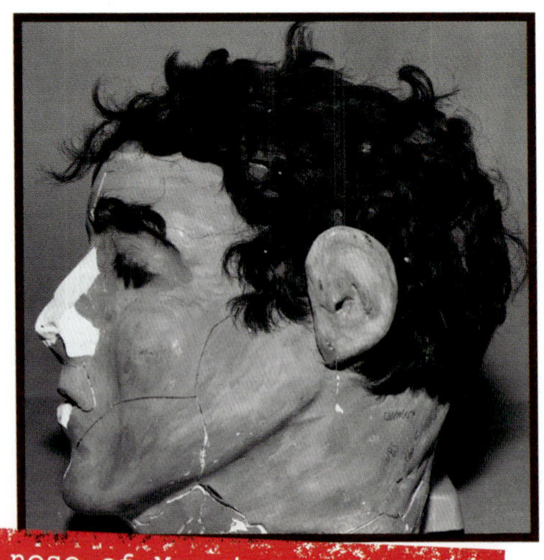

The nose of Morris's fake head broke when it hit the floor.

Alcatraz is now a popular museum. People can take tours inside. This is Frank Morris's cell.

CHAPTER 5

MANHUNT

It was the biggest manhunt in San Francisco history. No one reported a stolen car or clothes in the days that followed. Many people thought the escaped men probably drowned. But others believed the inmates got away. There was evidence that they escaped. A life raft was found on Angel Island the day after the men escaped.

These tools were recovered during the investigation.

There was more evidence that they had escaped. A childhood friend claimed to have seen the Anglin brothers. He ran into them in Brazil in 1975. He took a photo of them as proof. He asked the brothers how they escaped. They said they tied electrical wire to a ferry. The ferry left Angel Island at midnight.

This photo supposedly shows John and Clarence Anglin in Brazil.

The brothers held on to the wire behind the ferry. They rode it over to the mainland. In 1962, investigators had reported that wire was missing from the ferry's dock. The Anglin family also said they heard from the brothers after they escaped.

This is John and Clarence's sister, Marie. She holds up articles and images of her brothers.

CLUE OR COINCIDENCE?

A **freighter** reported seeing a body floating in San Francisco Bay on July 17, 1962. They said it was wearing jeans like the inmates wore. But they didn't stop to pick up the body. Was it one of the escaped men? No one knows. The body was never identified.

This freighter is entering San Francisco Bay. It is similar to the one from the 1962 report.

WHAT TO BELIEVE?

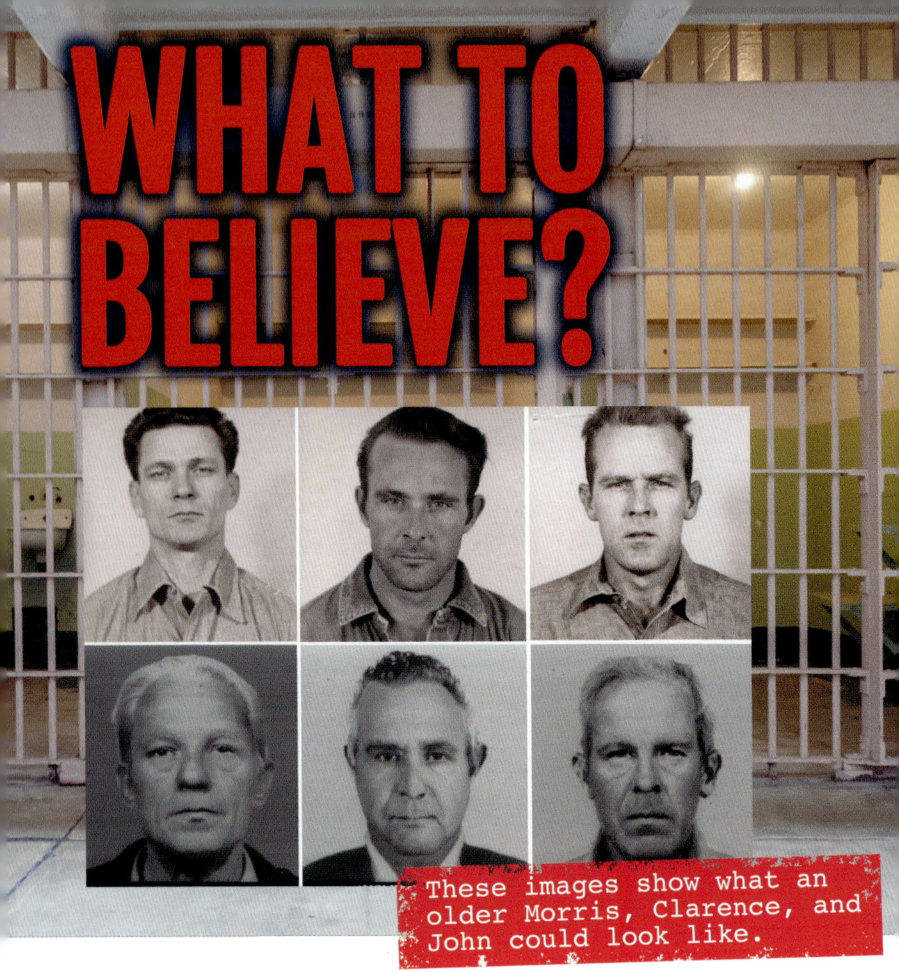

These images show what an older Morris, Clarence, and John could look like.

The FBI declared Morris and the Anglin brothers dead in 1979. But the US **Marshals Service** continued the investigation. They released images in 2022 of what the three men *could* look like. They would all be in their nineties. It's possible one or all of them are still alive.

Without enough evidence, the mystery may remain unsolved. What do you think? Maybe you're not sure. Maybe we'll never know if anyone really escaped from Alcatraz.

Alcatraz has about one million visitors each year. This sign is still there.

TIMELINE: Then and Now

Alcatraz Island opens as a federal prison.

The Battle of Alcatraz occurs.

A freighter spots a body in the bay.

1934 | 1937 | 1946 | JUNE 11 1962 | JULY 17 1962

Theodore Cole and Ralph Roe break out and disappear.

Frank Morris and Clarence and John Anglin escape.

Alcatraz Island opens to the public as a museum.

US Marshals Service releases images of what the three escaped inmates could look like.

1963 | 1973 | 1975 | 2022

Alcatraz prison closes.

A photo claiming to be of John and Clarence Anglin is taken in Brazil.

ONE CRIMINAL, THREE ESCAPES

Sometimes a prisoner refuses to stay in prison! Pascal Payet went to prison in France in 1997. He was sentenced to thirty years for murder during a robbery. He escaped in 2001 by **hijacking** a helicopter. Two years later, he broke three inmates out of the same prison. Again, he used a hijacked helicopter. Pascal was caught and put back in prison. He escaped one more time in 2007. Can you guess what Pascal was picked up in? A hijacked helicopter. He was finally caught in Spain and remains in prison. The authorities keep his location secret. They don't want anyone to try to break Pascal out again!

Pascal Payet in 2001.

GLOSSARY

cellblock (SEL-blahk) a group of prison cells that make up a section of a prison

FBI Federal Bureau of Investigation, principal investigative agency of the federal government of the United States

federal (FED-ur-uhl) in a country with a federal government, such as the United States, several states are united under and controlled by one central power or authority; each state also has its own government and can make its own laws

freighter (FRAY-tur) a ship or plane that carries cargo

hijack (HYE-jak) when someone takes illegal control of a vehicle or plane and forces its pilot or driver to go somewhere

inmate (IN-mate) a person in prison or a hospital

lockdown (LAHK-doun) a time when people must stay locked inside because there is potential danger

Marshals Service (MAHR-shuhls SUR-vis) principal federal law enforcement agency of the United States government

sentence (SEN-tuhns) a punishment given to someone who has been found guilty in court

INDEX

A

accordions, 23
Alcatraz Island, 6
Alcatraz prison
  air vents of, 24, 26, 31, 33
  description of, 4–5
  escape attempt in 1937 from, 8–11, 44
  escape attempt in 1946 from, 12–19, 44
  escape attempt in 1962 from, 20–40, 42, 44, 45
  front door of, 16, 17
  gun gallery of, 14–15
  location of, 4, 6
  main hallway of, 8
  as museum, 37, 43, 45
  nickname of, 7
  number of escape attempts from, 7
  privileges in, 23
  roof of, 30–31, 35
  sign of, 43
  unguarded hallway of, 24–25, 26, 30
  workshop of, 10
Angel Island, 35, 38, 39
Anglin, Clarence, 22–40, 42, 44, 45
Anglin, John, 22–40, 42, 44, 45
Anglin, Marie, 40

B

Battle of Alcatraz, 18–19, 44

C

Capone, Al, 5
Carnes, Clarence, 13, 14, 19
cellblocks, 14, 17
Cole, Theodore, 8–11, 44
Coy, Bernard, 12–19
Cretzer, Joe, 13, 14, 18, 19

F

fake bodies, 29, 32
fake heads, 28–29, 32, 36
FBI, 36, 42
federal, 5
freighters, 41, 44

G

gun gallery, 14–15

H

hijack, 46
Hubbard, Marvin, 13, 14, 19

I

inmates, 5

L

life jackets, 27, 35
lockdowns, 36

M

Marshals Service, 42, 45
Morris, Frank Lee
  accordion of, 23
  cell of, 37
  childhood of, 20
  crimes committed by, 20–21
  declared dead by FBI, 42
  escape from Alcatraz, 32–41, 44
  escape plan by, 22–31
music, 23

P

paddles, 27, 34
Payet, Pascal, 46
Popular Mechanics, 27
prison jobs, 9, 12
privileges, 23

R

rafts, 27, 34
Roe, Ralph, 8–11, 44

S

San Francisco Bay, 4, 6, 7, 38, 41, 44
sentences, 19
Shockley, Sam, 13, 15, 19

T

Thompson, Miran, 13, 14, 19

U

US Coast Guard, 36
US Marines, 18–19

W

West, Allen Clayton, 22, 24, 33, 36

ABOUT THE AUTHOR

Dinah Williams, who loves all things spooky and mysterious, has written more than a dozen books for kids, including *Amazing Immortals*; *Terrible but True: Awful Events in American History*; *True Hauntings: Deadly Disasters*; *Spooky Cemeteries*, which won a 2009 Children's Choice Book of the Year Award; and the Unsolved series: *Amelia Earhart*, *Bigfoot*, *Captain Kidd's Treasure*, and *Pyramids of Egypt*.